Dancers

Dancers

Ballet Paintings and Drawings

Donald Hamilton Fraser

Phaidon · Oxford
in association with
CCA Galleries

To Judy

Phaidon Press Limited, Musterlin House, Jordan Hill Road, Oxford OX2 8DP

First published in 1989

© 1989 Introduction, Nicholas Usherwood
© 1989 Text and pictures, Donald Hamilton Fraser

A CIP catalogue record for this book is available from the British Library.

ISBN 0 7148 2581 6

Designed by Jo Johnson
Typeset by Wyvern Typesetting Ltd, Bristol
Printed in England by Henry Stone and Sons (Printers) Limited, Banbury

Acknowledgements

Portrait of Mr B., Lincoln Kirstein, Ballet Society Inc., New York (1984).

The publishers wish to thank the CCA and private individuals who lent pictures for reproduction in this book. All the works are in private collections.

Note: All sizes are approximate and in inches.

1. Half title page: *Sketch: Contemporary Dance Inc.* Chalk and pencil, 1989. (5 × 3).

2. Frontispiece: *Study of dancer's feet.* Oil and pencil, 1986. (20 × 16).

3. Title page: *Dancer.* Chalk, 1987. (23 × 18).

4. Contents page: *Dancer with clasped hands.* Chalk and pencil, 1989. (19 × 13).

Contents

5. *Ballet school study.* Oil and chalk, 1987. (18 × 24).

Introduction

'Ballet is a graveyard for artists,' Donald Hamilton Fraser once remarked to me, and looking at the work of most contemporary painters of ballet, as well as of the history of the art over the last hundred years or so, the truth of this comment is sadly unavoidable. If it does not go off into the illustrational and kitsch – the usual problem – it tends to simplify and abstract to the point at which the dance itself becomes a secondary matter. Only Degas (one of Hamilton Fraser's great heroes, a sepia photograph of whom hangs in his studio as a kind of reminder) managed to steer a course between the two, and Hamilton Fraser's perceptive comments in this volume on how fierce a battle between sentiment and objectivity it had been even for him illuminates precisely the problems that still face any artist tackling the subject today. For, though you cannot draw or paint the ballet effectively without an intimate knowledge of it, as soon as you achieve that you tend to become so bound up in the intense and subtle magic of its disciplines that you can easily lose control of your own essential need for artistic detachment.

Hamilton Fraser's awareness of this dilemma is, in a sense, one of his greatest strengths, and infuses all the drawings and watercolours in this book. He certainly knows his ballet, having spent many years watching the English National Ballet in practice (quite astoundingly, Degas was very rarely allowed the same kind of privilege) and two years, back in the 1950s, writing about dance regularly for various magazines. He still writes passionately well about it, as his commentary shows, and he follows it closely, including regular visits to the Soviet Union. Yet, as he reveals here, he is only too well aware of the often tedious reminiscing of the balletomane and there is little of that apparent in his visual approach to the subject. At the same time, he is, of course, a highly trained professional artist with 25 years teaching painting at the Royal College of Art behind him and this high level of involvement in both art forms has left him with the feeling that ballet and fine art are parallel disciplines. Ballet for him is the three-dimensional equivalent of painting or, as he puts it, 'dancers can draw like Rodin, but they do it with their bodies', and the problem lies in the translation of this from one medium to the other.

His particular concerns are not dissimilar to those of Degas, the vast bulk of his work concentrating on practice and the behind-the-scenes aspects of ballet rather than the actual final performance. This is because he sees classical dance as a precise language and that in 'class' and the daily routine of rehearsal this language 'in its barest essentials, without embellishment, its syntax clear' is established. Such an approach also helps to explain why most of his dance subjects take the form of drawing, whether in charcoal, pastel or watercolour, rather than painting, for it is in the bold physical movements and sparseness of this medium that he finds the equivalent to the dancer's daily class. He likes to take the analogy further, commenting on how, just as a dancer has to practise every day, so he finds he needs the daily routine of drawing if he is not to become stiff and rusty.

In their expressive flowing quality and virtuoso technical skills, these drawings are very different from the brilliantly coloured semi-abstract qualities of his landscape paintings. He regards his ballet pictures as representing a quite separate activity, one that quite simply could not have been tackled in his painting style. This attitude stems from his strong feeling that in ballet painting the subject is a key element, and that, as he once put it to me, 'you can't put corners on dancers, and you must not break up their shape'.

This raises some tricky issues, for over-concentration on subject matter could so easily have led him back into those dangerous areas of illustration and kitsch alluded to earlier. In the event, he walks the tightrope between the two, with a very considerable degree of success, his sound training and the instincts it has bred in him keeping him well balanced. In this context, he likes to quote Pasternak: 'I see meaning in art not as an aspect of form, but as a hidden part of content.'

The integrity of the drawings also has much to do with the way in which he has worked to achieve them in the first place. Drawing in the practice studios is at the heart of it but he also has to make use of photography. Unlike, one suspects, many of his contemporaries, he is, however, very cautious about how he uses it. He basically distrusts the camera ('a liar'), but finds photography an important and necessary *aide-memoire* helping him to elucidate sequences of dance that his eye is not quick enough to follow. And, interestingly in this context, he finds he gets anything useful only from photographs he has taken himself where he has seen the movement with his own eyes and has already made certain choices about what the camera is recording. Other people's photographs are interesting, but basically useless to him. There is, too, the important fact that the camera is essentially a tonal instrument, whereas his drawings are, by their very nature, linear.

Photography has one other crucial practical function to perform for him – if he has a position he is interested in, a picture can show the dancer the particular position he requires. As he remarks, 'I'm not in the position of demonstrating dance steps to dancers!'

Ultimately though it comes down to the quiet coordination of eye and hand, pencil and notebook, and remaining as unobtrusive as possible, while he tries to capture those extraordinary and elusive moments of contrast between the ordinariness of dancers away from the actual business of ballet and the way in which they seem to light up from within when they are once again engaged with the dance. He is 'hooked by the extraordinary way in which the language of ballet confers sheer physical beauty on a person'. He enjoys, too, the actual physical aspect of the studio, the geometry of bars and mirrors within it, forming a highly pleasing frame-work within which the dancers can introduce their three-dimensional shapes and rhythms.

It is perhaps at heart the controlled, formalized movement which intrigues him so much about dance. In this it is like sport, another area which has been neglected by artists, and it may well be that dance will, perhaps, always stay the same way, too. Yet Donald Hamilton Fraser, by refusing to accept the idea that it is not possible to join the two areas of his life that he most cares about, has shown that it is still possible to produce works which can please balletomane and art lover alike.

Nicholas Usherwood

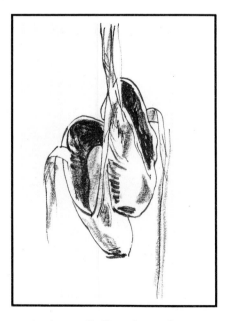

6. *Dancer's shoes.* Chalk and pencil, 1989. (6 × 4).

7. *Dancer putting on a shoe.* Oil and chalk, 1985. (24 × 18).

Dancers

Extracts from a Ballet Notebook

'Ballet is inexplicable.' Balanchine's remark haunts anyone who tries to write about classical dance. Perhaps that is why I choose to draw dancers – drawings that are little maps of experience. How often I say about something or the other, 'I cannot explain, give me a bit of paper and I'll draw it for you.'

For Balanchine ballet was a feminine form – 'without women there would be no ballet'. Even though the language of classical ballet was invented by men – Vestris, Noverre and Blasis – the muse of dance is female. The poet Gautier knew this when he conceived Giselle. The muse had her hand upon his heart and placed the feminine once and for all at the centre of the art of ballet.

No dancer can reveal her true stature until she has danced Giselle. The artistic health of a company is only as sound as its last production of it. My life seems to have been measured by the handful of great Giselles that I have seen, dancers who have found the sweetest flowering of their art in that dear, frail, old pantomime.

A dancer who has been a great Giselle carries a shadow of that poor, betrayed girl somewhere in her nature long after her dancing years are past. I remember, a few years ago, when I was haunting the fringes of a Bolshoi season in Paris, Anton Dolin said to me one evening, 'Come into the foyer and I'll introduce you to Chauviré'. I hardly dared believe him but there she was, an aloof, intimidating woman in her sixties – beautiful as ever. As I paid my compliments she listened politely and stared disconcertingly at me, and the very Giselle that had moved the ground under my feet at the Opera thirty years earlier gazed darkly at me. I swear it. Call it overactive imagination, but I have seen that same dark, lost look in other supreme Giselles – in Beriosova, Bessmertnova, Ulanova, Fracci Kirkland. Gautier released a wandering spirit when he conceived Giselle.

When two people look at the same thing they do not necessarily see the same thing. One looks with the eyes and sees with the mind. All seeing is subjective. In watching ballet I am acutely aware of this.

Like all painters, I am engaged in a continuous dialogue, not to say argument,

11

with my eyes. The problem is how to disregard what I think I see to make way for the actual evidence of my eyes. The task is hard enough when the object of one's scrutiny stays more or less in one place, but when it is moving as fast as a dancer that time between looking and seeing becomes hopelessly compressed. One looks at the dancer and sees *glissade*, looks down at the paper up again and sees *developpé*, down, up and it is *relevé* then *fouetté*, and so on until one is dazed by frustration and the page is covered with unconnected marks. No wonder that a sharp visual memory is the key attribute of a ballet artist.

Take a movement that may last just a few seconds. The dancer would accurately define it as, perhaps, *grand fouetté en tournant* ending in *attitude croisée*. She can describe it and she can do it. But the artist cannot describe in drawing the few million bits of visual debris that are transmitted from eye to brain as he watches her do her spin. He must try as best he can to summarize the meaning of the movement, the drawing becoming really a kind of metaphor, somehow implying the spacetime element by a degree of ambiguity of line and form and by the dynamics of the actual marks on the paper. This is a particularly seductive brick wall to beat one's head against and I suppose I shall go on doing it although the temptation to close the sketchbook, sit back and just enjoy the dancing is hard to resist.

An artist's experience of his own drawing is far removed from what someone sees when looking at the finished work. As it grows under his hand from the blank page it makes its own space, just as a dancer creates her own space in an *enchaînement* across a stage. The drawing, as it emerges moves in time, as does the dance, and should finally preserve this sense of unfolding in the tension of line and the quality of touch. Rodin was a master of this. He drew with time, hence the mysterious liquid space in which his subjects are contained. Inevitably he was obsessed by the subject of dance.

Dancers can draw with their bodies like Rodin but alas, their drawings evaporate as fast as they are created. To spend a day in a rehearsal studio watching Sevillano work on her Juliet is, for me, as awe-inspiring as it would have been to have watched Rodin drawing his Javanese dancers in the garden at Meudon.

I have often felt there was a good deal of nonsense in the description of Degas as a cold, aloof misogynist. Anyone who can read a drawing can see that the opposite is true, that he was, in fact, a man of passionate tenderness. Perhaps the draughtsman's discipline is mistaken for detachment; but the touch of the chalk on the paper, the modelling of an arm, the curve of a knee are eloquent of a more than willing submission to the subject, especially to the dancers.

He knew that a lethal vein of sentimentality had to be kept at bay if the tension of the drawings was not to be betrayed. This vulnerability shows in the poems that he wrote and in a recurring confessional note in his letters. But what misogynist would write of 'my little dears' of the Opera Ballet 'the dancers who have sewn this heart of mine into a bag of pink satin, pink satin slightly faded like their dancing shoes.' No wonder he put up defences.

Degas was probably the first major artist to allow photography to play a significant role in the process of his work. However, prudent man that he was, he kept the beast well chained. Although I seldom agree with what a photograph tells me it is interesting to know the point of view. All artists come to the realization, sooner or later, that the camera is a liar; but, as with all liars, it is wise not to let on that one has rumbled its compulsive falsehoods, just learn to discern the truth that lies behind the pattern of mendacity. It requires patience and much cunning to deal with this false friend.

A good many painters have turned to the subject of dance at some stage or other but, with a very few great and grand exceptions, the results have been dismal, bringing out the worst side of the artist, magnifying his limitations and advertising his deficiencies. Why do we fail? Is it for the same reason that painting always founders over any attempt to approach music directly as a subject? With music the reason is not hard to find; it is simply the invisibility of music that renders it firmly unamenable to even the most inspired visual metaphor. Yet perhaps, paradoxically, dance is as 'invisible' as music and in reality occupies that metaphysical realm 'over and above the senses'. Although the dance inhabits and surrounds the dancer it is not the dancer, its reality lying somewhere in ourselves as we watch.

Sixty odd years ago a young man called Sewell Stokes was invited by Isadora Duncan to a private performance in the huge dilapidated studio in Nice that was her home during the last years of her life. She was to dance just for Stokes and a friend who accompanied him. Since neither visitor played the piano it was decided that she would dance to the music of Wagner played on the gramophone. In these unpromising circumstances Stokes experienced – and for him it was for the first time – the phenomenon that had so moved audiences all over the world and given cause for even tough and critical witnesses like Stanislavsky to dissolve in admiration. The following year Stokes described in his book on Duncan his reaction to what he had seen that afternoon in Nice, and in doing so gives one of the most eloquent of all insights into the metaphysics of the dance:

I had no idea from which of Wagner's operas the record was made. But the solemn tune sounding in that great room like the lost lament of a dying prima donna did not seem to matter much. Nothing mattered when Isadora danced except her dance. She herself did not matter. One forgot, watching her move very slowly, that she was there at all. She drove out of the mind, with one slight movement of her foot or of her hand, the impression one had had a short time before of a large red-headed woman drinking lager beer. Her largeness, with everything else about her, disappeared. In its place was a spiritual vitality that defied the body it animated. Her dance, one felt, had been in that room since the beginning of time. It would be there until the end of time; a beautiful vibration that was eternally avoiding imprisonment. But somehow Isadora's body, for the few minutes when she moved it to the music, had captured that vibration. Through the medium of herself it was materialized.

The dancer and the dance remain one of the deepest mysteries of art, certainly defying the importunate gaze of the painter. But some of us will never learn from experience and allow ourselves to be drawn back again and again to the same glistening quicksand.

Inessa Dushkevitch, Principal Ballet Artist of the State Order of Lenin Academic Bolshoi Theatre of Opera and Ballet of the Byelorussian Soviet Socialist Republic. We had arranged to meet that morning at nine thirty in the Director's room. But who, I wondered, was this doe-eyed waif in jeans and T-shirt poking her head nervously round the door? Could it possibly be the same Dushkevitch who had stormed her way through *Spartacus* the night before, commanding every inch of the vast stage of the Minsk Opera House. Indeed it was the very same, but the golden flower-laden vision of yesterday's curtain calls was now a shy and diffident Cinderella back from the ball. The transformations in the lives of dancers never fail to startle me.

Over dinner, after the previous night's performance, Valentin Yelisariev, Minsk's ballet-master, had replied to my comment that she was one of the finest young dancers of her generation by saying, 'All right, she's all yours for half an hour before class tomorrow.'

So there she was, looking questioningly at me. 'How would you like to work?' she asked. All the inherent impossibilities of drawing throw me into a state of generalized panic when confronted by such opportunities. How could I ever have deluded myself into believing that I could really draw? Thirty minutes to unravel a secret, explore a paradox, describe the invisible. It would be so easy to throw it

14

8. *Inessa Dushkevitch rehearsing Juliet.* Oil and chalk, 1988. (24 × 18).

all away on a few contrived poses, a few hasty sketches that could have been done in the studio at home. That was a mistake that I had made before. Inessa rescued me by saying simply 'Would you just like me to dance a little for you?'

She put on her pointe shoes, bundled up her hair and, miraculously, Cinderella was back at the ball. The Dushkevitch of the night before grandly re-emerged as, silently, and with rapt absorption she showed me a series of beautiful paraphrases of the major repertoire – Aurora, Odette, Kitri, Giselle, Phrygia. She became each in turn and, as she danced, every note of the absent music was implicit in her. It was my thirty minutes with Terpsichore and I blessed the luck that had brought me to that unlikely encounter.

Dancers like Inessa Dushkevitch, mysteriously carrying within themselves – in the very substance of their flesh and bones – the entire art of classical dance, can summon up a whole theatre in a bare and silent room. 'I hope you found that useful', she said as she ran off to class.

Drawing dancers and looking at them so closely – that beautiful seventh vertebra that gives expression to the neck; the particular density of the tendon behind the knee; the degree of curve on the instep of the stretched foot; the ever changing conundrum of the upper back – I can never forget that dancers' bodies are the sole apparatus of their art; their obsession and their instrument; their palette, keyboard and lexicon.

Ballet is full of mysteries. Take the question of dancers' health. Before company class starts every day at ten o'clock they straggle in, drawn and ashen-faced. How it alarms me. I put it down to their diet of black coffee, chocolate bars and cigarettes. Poor girls, how could they have even managed the stairs let alone survive an hour or two of class. They line the studio with bags and bundles that disgorge a cargo of bandages and woollies, plasters and cotton wool. It is less a dance studio and more a casualty ward as they pad and plaster bruised feet, tie scarves like tourniquets around their heads and waists, heave themselves into plastic trousers – gingerly lest they awaken past injuries. As they hobble about I wonder how these invalids will ever bear the rigours of the barre.

Then, against all reason, a daily miracle takes place. As the first notes of the piano are struck, far from wilting they begin to shimmer with well-being. Their eyes open wider, their hair starts to shine, their skin glows and, as the time for centre work arrives the general radiance is dazzling. The miracle is that they are drawing strength from the very act of dancing itself, living off it, and nourished by it. As a long day of rehearsal passes the energy drawn from the dance seems to grow until the accumulated vitality is offered to their evening audience as an incomparable gift.

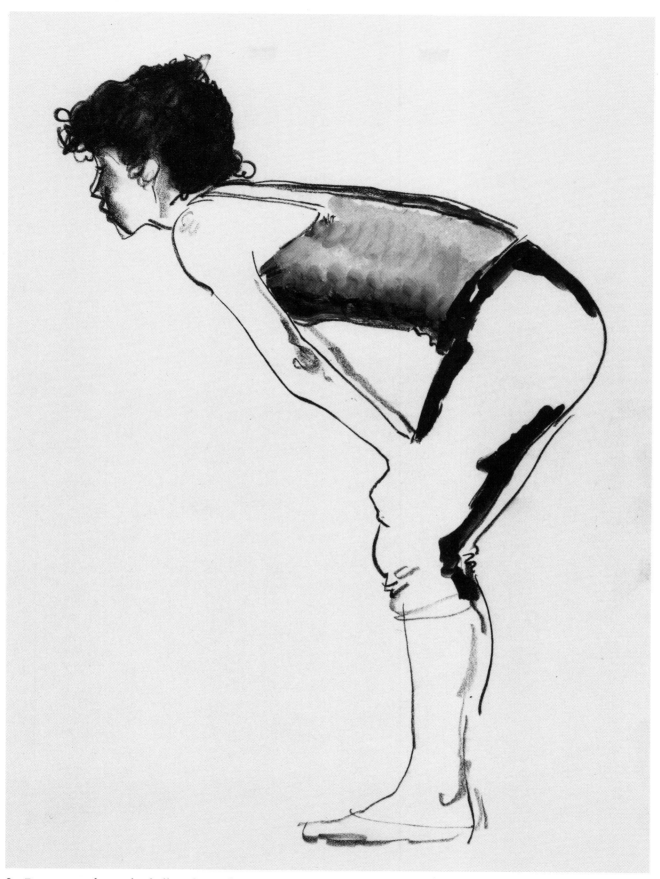

9. *Dancer at rehearsal.* Chalk and pencil, 1985. (22 × 15).

'If a dancer misses one day of class it is noticeable only to her; if she misses two days it is noticeable to those around her; but if she misses three days she can no longer be allowed to go on stage for then everyone will notice.' Those words of the Kirov's ballet-master are unequivocal – class is everything and dancers are reborn through it every day. So aware are they of that reality that, at the end of class, they always say thank you for it with a round of applause. Dancers would never dream of omitting this graceful gesture for throughout their training they will have ended every day's class with *le révérence*, a passage of beautifully constructed obeisances to the taker of the class. Though half blinded by sweat and gasping for breath ballet students always invest this moment with a touching gravity for they are showing their respect for the art of ballet as much as for their ballet master or mistress. The *révérence* is an act of genuine humility and confirms classical ballet as the most civilized and civilizing of arts.

The concept of the integration of mind and body, and the full consciousness of that integration, lies at the heart of classical ballet. It is an exact discipline of the soul in which daily class is as important to the dancer as the canonical hours are in the life of a convent. Though the dancer has one rest day a week a price is paid for even that one day.

'On Mondays,' Natasha said to me, 'I make class pay particular attention to *assemblées* in allegro section. Maintaining correct turnout of feet and hips in the fifth position is so helpful in re-establishing the unity of the inner and outer person.'

My admiration for classical dancers and the extreme discipline of their art is so intense that it surprises even me at times. Surprise succeeded by moments of doubt. Perhaps one is being foolishly idealistic or in thrall to some crazy illusion. A relief then to be reassured by reading Lincoln Kirstein again, New York's wise man of the dance.

'A particular psychic tempering, a peculiar anatomical configuration.' Yes, he understands dancers better than most and writes about them and '. . . their academy of physical, visible magic' with insight and passion:

> The ballet dancers' mode of existence may seem to outsiders as circumscribed as that of the convent or cloister. More than accepting rude discipline, professionals must endure not only unappeasable mental anxiety like everyone else, but also from their bodies, brittleness, strain, and fatigue. The hazards of a snapped Achilles tendon, bad sprains, slipped discs, the anguish and boredom of measureless recuperation, the slow and dubious resumption of practice and performances – these are taxes that every good dancer must pay. In this process, by the conscious

use and comprehension of suffering, the dancer begins to perceive the essence of the nature of existence, of being, of serving one's art and craft, of one's true nature and destiny. It is a stringent education, but when we see a great dancer on stage, performing with full power, we are inspecting a very developed human being, one who knows more about self than any psychiatrist can suggest.

'Of course, you realize,' said my friend Natasha 'that one of the worst things that can happen to a girl who is at ballet school is to develop a big bust.' My initial impulse to smile was checked by the implications of her remark. She had touched on a cruel truth about the physical mercilessness of ballet and the impossible demands that it makes of dancers. To be a talented young person dedicated to the art only to be denied a career by a failure to match an abstract physical ideal is a bitter experience. Despite the predictive tests on entry to ballet school nature still has a habit of bringing unwelcome surprises.

Perhaps we ask too much. It is, after all, a daunting ideal that faces the young dancer. She must not be too short or too tall. She must be strong yet give the impression of delicacy. She must have unusual powers of concentration and a highly developed musicality. She must have complete mastery of a technique of fiendish difficulty and complexity. She must be highly motivated while tempered by a degree of humility and be prepared to work inordinately long and hard. There is also the need for physical and mental courage and the ability to cope with pain. As if that were not enough she must be perfectly formed and proportioned, have the soul of a poet and preferably be beautiful.

The moment you step through the door of any ballet institution you are aware of the same distant sound – a sweetly familiar cacophany in three parts. An elevated voice with a curious sing-song intonation is pitched against an overbright piano and accompanied by a staccato of muffled thuds. It is ballet class in progress and we are hearing its pulse.

When I am a guest in class I always experience a fellow feeling with the pianist as being the only other earthbound person in the room. And how admirable they are these dance accompanists – stokers in the engine room of art. Heroes and heroines every one. Bravely struggling to retain the tatters of their own musical sensibility they stop-go their way everyday along a *via dolorosa* of heavily accented mazurkas, polkas, and galops, desperately trying to read the teacher's mind while resisting an obsessive urge to overpedal. Drigo and Minkus, Czerny and Delibes flow from their aching fingers as they measure out the immensity of time between the first slow pliés at the barre to the strenuous six-eight rhythms of grand allegro. Class is at least as gruelling for them as it is for the dancers but with little of the reward; no wonder that when they finally arrive at their stately three four improvisation for *le réverence* a heartfelt quality creeps into their playing, born of utter relief.

Walking into a studio full of dancers preparing for class or rehearsal is not an experience that does anything for my self-esteem. They all seem so graceful, so good looking, and so young. I feel unnaturally beset by gravity and twice my usual size as I head anxiously for the piano corner. Here is Caliban intruding upon a realm of gold. Thoughts of beauty and the beast cross my mind and I wonder how I could have chosen to wear such unsuitable clothes. Dancers are a friendly lot, but nothing can dispel the sensation of being an elephant caught up in a herd of antelopes.

I camp in the lea of the thunderous piano, my forlorn bits and pieces arranged around me, and begin the task of capturing a little of the splendour of the dance. It really is as hopeless as a child trying to catch the diamonds from a Guy Fawkes sparkler and I am hampered by a sorry discrepancy of means – my little pile of chalks and oily paper to match their sprung and shining bodies. It is an unequal contest.

The way that dancers dress when they are in class and rehearsal shows a limitless originality, not to say eccentricity. Since costume has a tendency to define the form of the body it adorns, an artist in the ballet studio is faced by a situation of continuous anatomical revelation. The regulation leotard and tights of ballet school are long past, and dancers in a company indulge in a riot of invention which is all directed to the most practical of purposes; namely to concentrate heat to specific groups of muscles. From the more mature male dancer at the stage of playing kings and magicians, wedded to his stately dressing gown, to the newest lycra-clad member of the corps the sartorial range is wide. Mostly the men favour the simple solution of wearing three of everything, layers being the name of the game. The girls are particularly inventive in the use of woolly bits and pieces and seem to prefer everything either rolled up or, more precariously, rolled down. Billowy netherwear of what surprisingly appears to be polythene is popular, less so with the teacher, for it obscures the line; and I have made the delightful discovery that the art of crochet, which I had imagined to be long dead, lives on in a variety of little tops and so on worn by dancers.

Garments worn in the ballet studio can be ingeniously deployed. I remember one young dancer who gained a degree of privacy for herself when preparing for class by bending forward, grasping her ankles with her hands and with astounding suppleness pressing her forehead against her shins so that a gigantic cardigan that she always wore fell over her head like a tent, within

10. *Male dancer.* Chalk and pencil, 1987. (19 × 13).

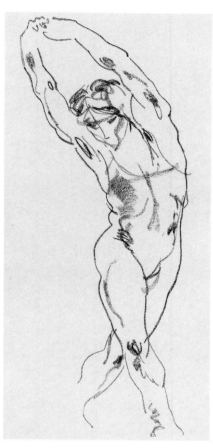

11. *Two dancers.* Chalk and pencil, 1987. (19 × 13).

12. *Sketchbook page.* Chalk and pencil, 1986. (24 × 14).

which she would remain in meditation for what seemed minutes at a time.

The colour of all this sluices out the eyes with turquoises layered on lime yellows, electric pinks on vibrant puces, emerald green on mustard, and since dancers wear anything and everything with sensational style the effect is one of surpassing beauty with which no designer collection could ever compete.

Sometimes when I look at my watch in the morning and notice that it is ten o'clock, I remember that at this particular hour in cities on every continent of the world a shared ritual is about to be enacted; a ritual virtually unaltered for two centuries. The chief celebrant of the rite will walk into a studio, or on to a stage and address those assembled in the language of the French eighteenth-century court. Ballet class will be in progress. From the first notes of the accompanying music, the ritual grows in complexity, proceeding unquestioned and with almost no deviation until the final *révérence*.

Class marks the start of every dancer's day and to 'do a good class' is to set that day on a successful course. This beautiful event has the quality of a secular liturgy, a celebration of the whole person, physical and spiritual. From the first notes of the accompanying music, four-bar phrases in six-eight time for *pliés*, this great canon of formal movement grows in complexity. *Battements tendus, battements glissés, ronds de jambe à terre, grands battements, adage* and so on, an unquestioned devotion culminating in the joyful elevation of *grand allegro*. Continuities such as this are the armour of civilization; a reassurance for an uncertain world.

It seems to me that the human race divides rather neatly into those who love ballet to distraction and those for whom it is entirely without meaning, with not much in between. For Alexandre Benois the rapture was immediate and permanent. Attending a performance of *La Bayadère* at the Maryinsky Theatre at the age of seventeen he was so overwhelmed that, as he later recalled, 'I actually fell ill with ecstasy and in my delirium raved of angels in muslin dresses.'

Of course, in my own cosmology, angels in tarlatan skirts are an entirely feasible proposition, but Benois knew that the corps de ballet at the Maryinsky were only mortals disguised as angels. How often, though, in this domain so peculiarly subject to miracles, have I had the fleeting conviction that a particular dancer is an angel cunningly disguised as a mortal.

But not everyone in St. Petersburg of the 1880's felt like Benois. There was a young friend of his, newly arrived from the provinces, who stubbornly held to the view that ballet was a senseless and derisory art form. Only slowly and painfully, under the glare of Benois' own passion, were his eyes finally prised open to the splendour of the dancer's art. The young man was Serge Diaghilev. So there we have the ultimate good news for those who find ballet meaningless and even rather embarrassing; they do not have to endure their benighted state forever – conversion is possible.

There was a time when the doors to paradise were generally made of brown, varnished wood with brass handles. But now as I grow older I find myself more often confronted by steel and glass. But my step still quickens as I approach them whether the way lies from Floral Street, Cour Haussmann or Petrovka. As all heavenly portals should be, the stage doors of the great opera houses are guarded by dragons; the angels come later.

That labyrinth of passages, lifts and staircases that lie around the central cavern of the stage is a never-ending adventure; the pervading atmosphere of dream acts like a drug. To be set free backstage in a big opera house is to me the best present in the world. Flattened against the wall by a surging flight of swans, I reflect glumly on the ordinariness of the world that waits outside.

The world is not so rich in choreographers that it can afford to ignore a genius whose work lies buried in the memories of Leningrad's dancers. Once ballet-master of the Kirov, Leonid Yakobson died in 1975 after a creative life made wretched by endless conflict with authority. One of the first duties of the *glasnost* era at the Kirov should be to research and preserve all that is possible from his output as a choreographer.

Film and videotape records exist on a very partial basis; in fact, I have been shown a complete tape of his astonishing and deeply controversial ballet *The Twelve* which was suppressed soon after its first performance. It is a major work which should have been re-instated in the Kirov repertoire years ago and hopefully soon will be, but most of his ballets are being allowed to slip away on the back of passing time.

Almost all that is known of his work in the West is the profoundly original miniature called *Vestris* in which a young Baryshnikov pole-axed a London audience one night nearly twenty years ago – he has rarely performed it since. Yakobsen was a remarkable choreographer and mentor to an outstanding generation of Kirov dancers who should now give a lead in retrieving and remounting his work.

I find intense pleasure in visiting little museums. The Haydn House in Eisenstadt, the Episcopal Museum in Vich, Vienna's Dommuseum, the Bourdelle museum in Paris, the Vasnetsov house in Moscow. They become old friends to look up whenever possible, but most beguiling of all are the tiny museums tucked away in Europe's great opera houses.

For the confirmed sentimentalist such places are best experienced in the dimmest of lights, the deepest quiet, absolute solitude and, preferably, late on a winter afternoon. Then perhaps one may catch just the faintest echo of lost voices from the fragile souvenirs resting in their graveyard of glass and mahogany.

The little museum of the Bolshoi, a few steps across Sverdlov Square from the theatre, still retains a proper reticence. The grandeur of the art nouveau staircase does little to offset the general air of faded domesticity that characterizes so many Russian institutions and the two rooms that house the collection are well concealed beyond an office where two languid young women pursue some suitably unspecific administrative task. The huge and heavy light of Moscow winter filters through the lace curtains and lies over the cases like a thin dusting of snow while the intense stillness seems like an invisible companion in the room. Libretti and letters, slippers and pointe shoes, feathers and fans; the solitary worshipper will find peace here. Opera costumes of insane complexity stand stiffly to attention, Khovanschina, Queen of Spades, Boris Godunov. Photographs of handsome men with broad brows and the well developed jaw muscles of the opera singer, women with dark and distant Russian eyes; one wonders what voices they offered to their adoring audiences all those years ago. Ballerinas' costumes, like children's dressing up clothes, forlornly virginal in their glass boxes, still bear – or is it only imagination – the faint outlines of the bodies that once inhabited them. The velvet and muslin of Kitri's dress worn by the great Lepeshinskaya in *Don Quixote*, the soft black of its bodice now tinged with grey, hangs beside the diaphanous little shift that Ekaterina Maximova wore on the night that she first danced Juliet under the proud eye of her mentor, Ulanova, almost thirty years ago. Such treasures are not for profane eyes.

In view of dance's origins in ritual it is appropriate that it was a priest who collected and listed the first few phrases of what was to become the language of classical ballet. In 1588 Arbeau's *Orchésographie* began by listing the three basic positions of the feet in court dances and by 1830 with Blasis' monumental *Code de Terpsichore* a comprehensive language was in place upon which all subsequent classical ballet has been based. This language of movement has an alphabet of forty seven positions, twenty six positions of the legs, seven positions of the torso, seven of the arms and seven of the head. The permutations of this alphabet, allowing for the factor of movement in space, offers a virtually limitless lexicon. Here, in its vocabulary grammar and syntax, is an astonishing means of abstract discourse rivalling the greatest of mathematical and musical constructs, an edifice of epic dimensions and one of the noblest achievements of the European mind.

What we call ballet today is a complex form. It is something like a river with its source in the pellucid waters of classicism flowing through various shoals and shallows of naturalism to the vast shifting delta of modern and post-modern dance. But the purity of the source can never be taken for granted; it must be defended and renewed as it follows its course through the bodies of individual dancers. The classical language is written in the flesh and bones of dancers; the legibility and grammatical purity of that writing has to be tested and examined every single day. The struggle to retain this pristine form is the reason why teachers and ballet-masters and mistresses bear such a heavy responsibility when they give daily class. Ballet, above all the arts, needs its teachers, its guardians of theory and practice: Johannson, Cecchetti, Vaganova, Preobrajenska, Volkova, Legat – without a rigorous teaching tradition classical ballet would be no more.

Mime as an essential part of ballet corresponds, in a way, to the use of recitative in opera. One cannot fail to be stirred by Wagner's huge, extended passages of instrumented recitative or by Verdi's way of making recitative bear the full weight of pathos in the approach to an aria; sudden fragments, dry except for a few murmuring chords as in Lady Macbeth's 'Nel di della vittoria' or delivered alongside the shadow of a melody in Violetta's wonderful 'Teneste la promessa'. Nobody would dream of tampering with such perfection. Yet in the great ballets like *Swan Lake*, *Sleeping Beauty* and *Giselle* mime, which gives texture to the whole as *recitativo secco* does in opera, has in recent years been treated too often with a shameful disregard, crucial passages of mime even disappearing altogether in some modern productions. It is a sad impoverishment.

It is a rare thing to find a ballet sustained with any authority by classical form alone. Most ballet is a troika of mime, colloquial and dramatic dance form and pure classical dance. In the best choreography these elements balance and complement each other by their distinct character. When they cease to define themselves in the overall texture of the work and become confused one with the other, as happens in a lot of contemporary ballet, both audience and dancers find themselves on soft and dangerous ground. They may enjoy the spongy feel of that ground but it could swallow them up in the end, and the whole art of ballet with them.

The late Arnold Haskell was a great scholar of the ballet and, as a young man, I hung upon his every word. He believed that each generation produces no more than half a dozen or so truly great classical dancers; and that every so often a generation draws a complete blank, giving cause for the anxious conviction that

25

the art of ballet is dying. In the fifty years since Haskell expressed that view the training of classical dancers has hugely increased as have the number of companies around the world. Yet although his figure of six should statistically now stand at around thirty six, I feel in my bones that nature is not that generous and the original figure is still nearer the truth.

Of the present generation of dancers the one who must come high on anyone's list is the Kirov's Altynai Asylmuratova. Apparently put together by a committee of angels, she seems to possess all the attributes that could conceivably be desired in a classical dancer. Yet it is not simply her dramatic power, her subtle radiance, her velvety yet supercharged technique or her flawless physical beauty which set her apart. It is, more importantly, the way that she expresses in herself the newness, the uniqueness, the modernity of her own generation's response to the tradition of classical ballet. She embodies the growing point of that tradition and, although the Kirov classicism and the Vaganova schooling is apparent from her head to her toes, when one watches her dance one knows more surely than by looking at a calendar that it is the last decade of the twentieth century. She is living evidence of why we can never, ever, describe a truly great dancer as 'another Ulanova or another Pavlova' or say that 'she is just like Fonteyn or just like Lepeshinskaya'. She will be showing us something that we have never seen before, something indefinable which has not existed before, something only of this particular time. Through dancers like Asylmuratova classical ballet recreates itself generation by generation.

Musicians can hear their music as they perform it, actors the lines that they speak, singers their song. Painters can see their paintings and writers read their words. The work is experienced by the shared senses of the creator and audience.

Yet although an audience experiences a dancer's movement through its eyes, that is a joy denied to the dancer herself, for when she is on stage it is she alone who cannot see her dance. Her awareness of it lies in her special sensitivity to the space displaced by her own body in movement. Gone is that stern critic, the mirror in the practice studio; gone the ballet-master's watchful eye by which she 'sees herself' in rehearsal. There, in performance, she has to rely on a radar of the nerves and muscles to measure the placing of her feet, the line of her back and arms, the position of her head upon her shoulders, the whole unseen structure of her dance. Her pleasure in that dance may be even greater than ours, but it is pleasure of a different and secret kind.

Watching a group of dancers getting ready for a rehearsal of *Swan Lake*, I marvelled for the thousandth time at how profoundly their simplest movements

13. *Dancer with raised arm.* Oil and chalk, 1987. (12 × 18).

of preening and stretching differed from the way that ordinary people use their bodies.

It is impossible to search for any definition of this difference through drawing unless one has some idea of how and why a dancer is physically altered and moulded by a classical training. Unless one understands the dancer's body one can never really understand the art of ballet which is, after all, made out of it just as a painting is made of paint and a poem of words. Eric Gill put it rather well when he said that 'one cannot draw something until one knows how it is made and what it is for'.

The teacher becomes a sculptor as she takes the pupil in her hands, and just as the sculptor will start a figure by working the clay on the armature from the centre, the re-making of the ballet student's body will be based on a particular alignment of the pelvis, moving upward to begin the lengthening of the sacral spine and downward through the inner thighs – the start of the dancer's famous turn-out. It is this carriage of the pelvis that will eventually determine the dancer's axial and gravitational integrity and her effectiveness in weight transference. It will govern the verticality of the spine as far as the head and the capacity for turn-out as far as the feet, and finally mediate in that exquisite dialogue between the back and the lower limbs which is so fundamental to the art.

These changes are only brought about slowly and painfully but, in the hands of a good teacher, the result can be a human being of real physical splendour, fluent in the classical vocabulary and capable of bearing the full burden of discourse in this beautiful three-dimensional tongue. As an onlooker I am fascinated by the process of ballet education and training, not just as a preparation for performance but as a form of knowledge in itself. I find this process spellbinding and a focus of gratitude that such severe discipline is borne so willingly in the cause of art.

In the eight or so years that it takes to create a classical dancer a significant physical change has to be effected, a progressive re-alignment of the muscular-skeletal structure of the growing body. The responsibility borne by the teacher in this is tremendous for not only is she teaching dance steps and technique, but she is actively shaping the body of the dancer to be. A mediocre teacher can only produce mediocre dancers, and it is certainly true that faults acquired early on are all but impossible to eradicate later.

Twentieth-century ballet is unimaginable without Stravinsky. No other major composer has ever devoted such a substantial part of his work to the ballet. From his great orchestral fire-storms that set European music ablaze at the beginning

14. *Coppelia*. Chalk
and pencil, 1987.
(21 × 11).

of the century to the austere serialism of his late work he did much to shape the course of his sister art.

Yet it may well be that the dance had, in its turn, a profoundly altering effect upon him and that his move towards formalism that followed after *Rite of Spring* may have been part of that effect. By then he was experiencing a greater familiarity with the language of purely classical ballet – he later even tried his hand at serious choreography in the original version of *Jeu de Cartes* – and that familiarity left an unmistakable imprint upon his mature work.

Throughout his so-called neo-classical period and beyond, the abstract and formal language of classical ballet is closely paralleled by the laconic, ordered harmonies and asymmetrical rhythms of his music. His insistence that his music did not 'express' anything other than its own form confirms that we can read it in the same terms as the inherently emotion free movements of classical dance.

Stravinsky's lean, aristocratic musical form is, in a sense, pure classical dance – a ringing challenge to the choreographer. It is no wonder that Balanchine responded so eagerly.

Because of this intense symbiotic relationship I am sure that if ever the great language of Noverre and Blasis, Petipa and Balanchine was somehow lost or forgotten – which Heaven forbid – it, or something very like it, could be re-invented from a visual projection of Stravinsky's musical forms, so close are they in spirit to classical ballet.

The little that I have learned about the theory and practice of ballet teaching during the time that I have been drawing dancers convinces me that the subject is one of considerable intellectual rigour. What excites me is that it is laterally a strictly finite subject yet one of infinite depth. Its study is conducted with passionate intensity, the subtlest differences assuming a huge significance that may take decades of argument to resolve. It is esoteric, it is precise, it is highly formalized and addresses an intriguing dichotomy of the material and the immaterial. To hear two of its major teachers arguing theory is to enjoy an experience even more nuanced than a pair of theologians discussing the Filioque controversy.

No other art depends so absolutely upon its teachers. The words 'self-taught' cannot exist in the vocabulary of classical ballet.

St. Augustine said that 'dance signifies and displays something over and above the senses'. Indeed it is unique in its capacity to accommodate the spiritual in the context of the physical. At its heart classical ballet seems to hold an inviolable

15. *'Nutcracker', Act I. Drosselmeyer.* Oil, 1987. (24 × 18).

space and when it offers its purest moments of illumination it is as if a layer is stripped from the physical world and, by the sudden transparency, I look into that space and sense an undisclosed treasure. The power of that inner space of ballet draws me back again and again.

I should like to express my thanks to all the dancers who, with much generosity, have allowed me to intrude upon their working life. I am especially grateful to English National Ballet for all the assistance the company has given to me over the years. I am also indebted to Natasha, Nadya and Zbyshek Lisak of the West Street Ballet School, London, for helping me in a number of ways.

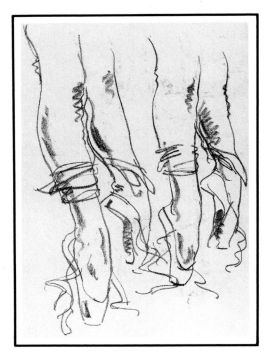

16. *Study of feet and legs.* Chalk and pencil, 1987. (19 × 13).

The Plates

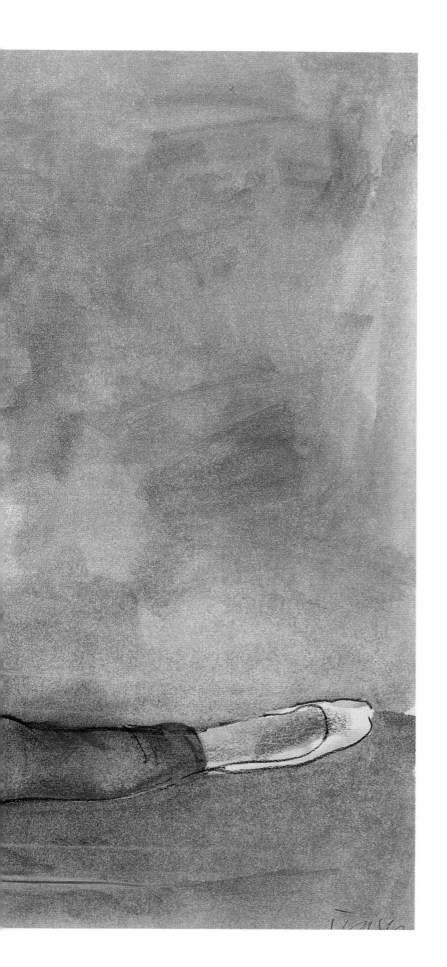

18. *Dancer pinning up hair.* Ink, 1985. (6 × 4).

17. *Seated dancer, red leg warmers II.* Oil and chalk, 1985. (18 × 21).

19. *Dancer at the barre.* Oil and chalk, 1987. (26 × 15).

20. *Dancer in class.* Oil and chalk, 1987. (24 × 15).

21. *Bearded dancer and friend at rehearsal.* Oil and chalk, 1987 (18 × 26).

22. *Dancer putting on a sock.* Oil and chalk, 1987. (23 × 18).

23. *Rehearsing Pas de Deux*. Oil and chalk, 1987. (24 × 18).

24. *Italian dancer.* Oil and chalk, 1986. (21 × 18).

25. *Dancer tying a shoe.* Chalk and pencil, 1987. (18 × 17).

26. *Dancer in class*. Oil and pencil, 1984. (28 × 19).

27. *Dancer in school.* Oil and chalk, 1986. (20 × 16).

28. *Dancer resting II*. Oil and chalk, 1985. (24 × 18).

29. *Rehearsal break.* Oil on paper, 1984. (24 × 18).

30. *Dancer dressing.* Screen print, 1988. (18 × 26).

31. *Dancer resting after class.* Oil and chalk, 1985. (12 × 10).

32. *Dancer*. Oil on paper, 1982. (21 × 20).

33. *Study of a dancer.* Chalk and pencil, 1987. (12 × 14).

34. *Seated dancer.* Oil and chalk, 1986. (24 × 15).

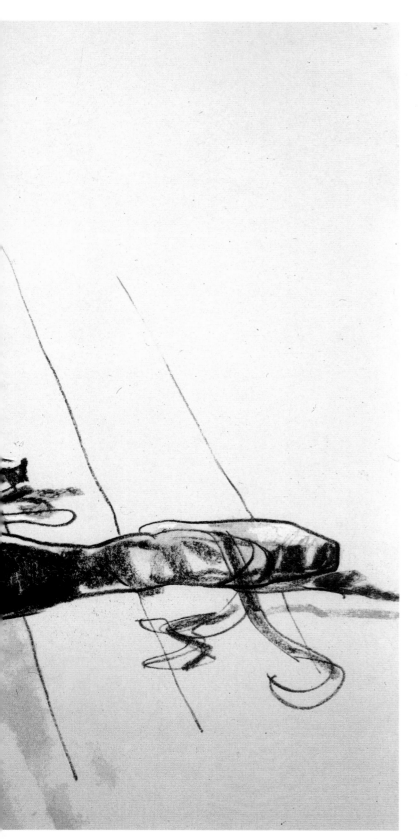

36. *Dancer adjusting her shoe.* Chalk and pencil, 1986. (19 × 13).

35. *Dancer tying her shoe.* Screenprint, 1988. (18 × 26).

37. *Dancer limbering.* Chalk and pencil, 1987. (25 × 18).

38. *Dancer in practice tutu.* Oil and chalk, 1987. (18 × 28).

39. *Dancer putting on a shoe.* Oil and chalk, 1987. (23 × 18).

40. *Dancer in pink tutu.* Oil and chalk, 1983. (22 × 18).

41. *Dancer rehearsing Tricorne.* Chalk, 1984. (20 × 16).

42. *Dancer rehearsing Juliet.* Oil and chalk, 1987. (24 × 18).

 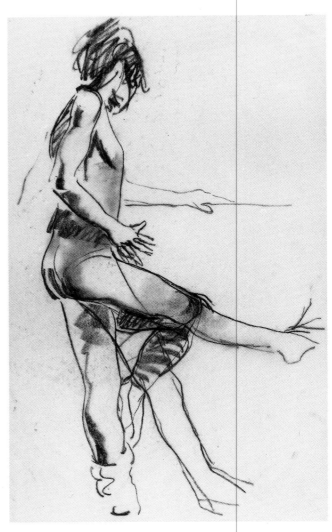

43. *Sketchbook page.* Chalk and pencil, 1986. (19 × 13).   **44.** *Classroom sketch.* Chalk and pencil, 1985. (19 × 13).

45. *Dancer adjusting her tutu.* Oil and chalk, 1987. (26 × 18).

46. *Dancer testing her shoes.* Oil and chalk, 1986. (24 × 17).

47. *Coppelia.* Oil and chalk, 1986. (22 × 15).

48. *Trinidad Sevillano and Matz Skoog rehearsing 'Romeo and Juliet'.* Oil and chalk, 1987. (24 × 18).

49. *Two dancers rehearsing.* Oil and chalk, 1987. (26 × 18).

50. *Study for Clara, 'Nutcracker'*. Oil and chalk, 1987. (26 × 17).

51. *Dancer rehearsing Romeo.* Oil and chalk, 1987. (24 × 18).

52. *Pas de Deux 'Romeo and Juliet'*. Oil and chalk, 1987. (26 × 20).

53. *Pas de Deux 'Meditation'*. Oil and chalk, 1987. (26 × 18).

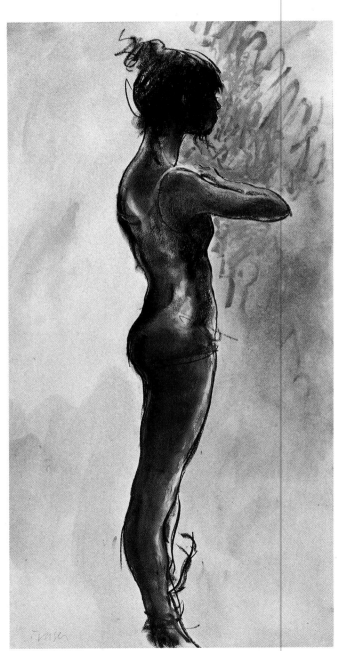

54. *Fouetté.* Chalk, 1989. (16 × 10).

55. *Dancer against the light.* Oil and chalk, 1986.
(26 × 18).

56. *Death of Mercutio, 'Romeo and Juliet'. Oil, 1987. (18 × 24).*

57. *Death of Mercutio, 'Romeo and Juliet'.* Oil, 1987. (24 × 18).

58. *Two pages holding a mirror, 'Romeo and Juliet'*. Oil and chalk, 1987. (26 × 16).

59. *The Nutcracker and Drosselmeyer.* Oil on paper, 1987. (24 × 17).

60. *Clara and the Nutcracker.* Oil, 1987. (23 × 18).

61. *Petrouchka.* Oil, 1984. (28 × 19).

62. *The Ballerina from 'Petrouchka'.* Oil, 1984. (28 × 19).

63. *Folkdancer*. Oil and chalk, 1984. (28 × 18).

Further Information

Donald Hamilton Fraser

Born 1929. Studied St. Martin's School of Art, London, 1949–50. Studied and worked in Paris. French Government Scholarship 1953–54. Taught at Royal College of Art 1957–83. Fellow of Royal College of Art 1970. Hon. Fellow 1984. Royal Academician 1985. Member of the Royal Fine Art Commission since 1986. Lives and works in Henley-on-Thames, Oxfordshire.

Individual Exhibitions:

Gimpel Fils Gallery, London. Nine shows 1953 to 1971.

Paul Rosenberg, New York. Eleven shows 1958 to 1978.

Galerie Craven, Paris. 1957.

Gimpel-Hanover Galerie, Zurich. 1967

Bohun Gallery, Henley, England. Five shows 1977 to 1988.

Scottish Gallery, Edinburgh. 1981.

Gallery Ten, London. Five shows 1980 to 1988.

Christie's Contemporary Art, London. 1985.

Christie's Contemporary Art, New York. 1985. Toured to Philadelphia, Kansas City, Tulsa, and other US cities.

CCA Galleries, London. 1987 to 1989.

Kingfisher Gallery, Edinburgh, 1988.

Selected Group Shows:

1953 British Romantic Painting in the 20th century. National Museum of Wales.

1954 British Painting. Whitechapel Art Gallery, London.

1957–58 Six British Painters. Arts Club, Chicago. Albright Gallery, Buffalo. National Gallery of Canada, Ottawa.

1963 British Art Today. Dallas Museum of Art. Santa Barbara Museum of Art. San Francisco Museum of Art.

1967 Pittsburgh International. Carnegie Institute, Pittsburgh.

1964 Englische Kunst der Gegenwart. Stadlische Kunstgalerie, Bochum, FRG.

1977 British Painting 1952–1977. Royal Academy, London.

1980 Ten British painters. Israel Museum, Jerusalem.

1983 International Print Biennale, Tai Pai.

Public Collections include:

Museum of Fine Arts, Boston, Massachusetts.

Albright-Knox Gallery, Buffalo, New York.

City Art Museum, St. Louis, Missouri.

Wadsworth Atheneum, Hartford, Connecticut.

Hirshhorn Museum, Smithsonian Institution, Washington DC.

Carnegie Institute, Pittsburgh.

Yale University Art Museum, New Haven, Connecticut.

National Gallery of Canada. Ottawa.

National Gallery, New South Wales, Melbourne.

Arts Council and many other British public and corporate collections.

Desert Art Museum, Palm Springs.

Index